The Refocus Challenge

A 40 DAY PERSONAL TRAINING GUIDE TO

Refocus. Revamp. Revitalize
YOU

By Robyn Robbins

ThriveHER
PUBLISHING HOUSE

Foreword By Melissa C. January

Whether you are an entrepreneur, teacher, coach or just an awesome individual, this book should be added to your "must read" list. I was delighted when I received a request from Robyn Robbins to write a brief foreword. For many years I admired her ambition, drive to overcome and achievements by simply using a pen.

This volume serves as a great introduction on how to refocus, revamp and revitalize yourself in 40 days. Daily assignments will allow you time to reflect on self and areas that need your attention. This 40-day Challenge is more than just a book.

REFOCUS- REVAMP- REVITALIZE- YOU...

Looking through this magnificent read, I am confident whether relationally, business, mentally, physically, or spiritually these daily tools and keys will help you unlock and break cycles in your life.
This is a book of transformation and courage. Robyn's message is challenging but filled with encouragement to inspire the reader to reach higher and take life to the next level. Read it, enjoy it, and learn from it.

Sincerely,

Melissa January
Certified Life Coach
MEKEI International Coaching LLC
Suwanee, GA

PREFACE

This book was birthed out of my ambition and drive to overcome the ruts and cycles in my life and the desire to revamp and locate myself. During that time, I earnestly began to seek help and assistance from God. Each day He would prompt my spirit to do a task.

I began to notice after about 3 days that I was in a divine process. The breakthrough that I experienced was phenomenal and so liberating! It is my sincere hope that this book and its activities help to do the same for you! In and through this book you will have the opportunity to look at, examine, and be completely honest with self in order to see the results you desire in your life.

It doesn't matter which area of your life, whether it be relation, business, mentally, spiritually, and or physically that you are looking to "revamp or refocus" these daily tools and keys will help unlock and or assist you to get you there!

I would like to give a big special thanks to the ThriveHer publishing House team, Melissa January and Sheryl Tillage. You all have done a phenomenal Job contributing to this work and it has been a blessing!

The Psychology Behind The Book

Most know how this book came about and how at first, I didn't realize exactly what was taking place. What I did not realize was that what the Spirit of God was leading me to do not only had biblical principles but psychology behind it as well. Although this book gives a combination of making decisions, purging from the excess and or the negative it also fosters an environment to help break or make new habits in order to break those ruts or cycles we sometimes experience.

So, I began to research and read up on some things. First allow me this disclaimer: I am not a psychologist. I am one that does believe in adequate research from reputable sources. I have formed my own perspective based on my faith, research and the research of actual psychologists.

Here is what I've realized:

In this book, through this training we are subconsciously making and breaking habits. We are replacing old habits with new healthier habits that will catapult us in the direction we desire to go. Eventually giving the foundation or support needed to reach our goals. However, consistency is key in order to produce positive results.

Per my research we have been mislead by the myth that it takes 21 days to break or make a habit. This is false and has been misunderstood for quite some time. This notion derived from Dr.Maxwell Maltz but he didn't say it takes 21 days he said based on his study a minimum of 21 days. However, like the game telephone words get left out as time goes on and we tend to believe what we hear if it's said enough.

The truth is that it varies based on the person, their circumstances, and the kind of behavior they desire to break or make. It takes time to adjust and for the new behavior to become automatic. So how long does it actually take you ask?

Based on Phillipa Lally a health psychology researcher's study at University College London on average it takes 66 days or over 2 months for the new behavior to be automatic or feel natural. Don't worry or fret my friend remember great things are a result of hard work and that great things are never instant!

Lucky for us this only makes up 30-40% of the book. The rest is based on your commitment and willingness to do the work, be consistent and making the necessary decisions that will assist you in purging from those negative places, people, or things to get to where you want to go.

Remember this friend, this book can be done as often as you need and can be applied to different areas of your life. You are on a beautiful journey and I commend you! It takes a special kind of person to strive for what they want in and out of life and I'm happy to say that person is You!

INTRODUCTION

What you need:

You will need a pen and a set time in which you set aside to do this challenge and its activities. Are you ready? Let's begin! Remember to be consistent throughout and apply, apply, apply!

How it works:

If you have purchased an e-book instead of a paperback, you will need to Purchase a notebook specifically for this training. It helps to have a visible record of your progress.

You will have challenges 4 days a week (Mon-Thurs), during that time you do the work and complete the challenges in addition to journaling your thoughts and feelings during the process.

During the weekends you will have what we call a "Time of Reflection" (Fri-Sun). During your time of reflection, we look over the week, complete anything we didn't complete, tie up any other loose ends and check to see if your overall goal was met for the week.

Other Books by Robyn Robbins

"Diaries of An Ex-Adult Entertainer: My Road to Redemption"

"Daddy's Little Girls: Daughters of God" A Book of Healing

"ThriveHer Getting Back 2 You!"

"ThriveHer Getting Back 2 You Reflect Purge Plan Journal"

Coming soon:

"Esther's Oil: Preparing for Destiny"

What is Success?

As a Master Coach, I often ask my clients this question. It is very important to define the word success because of the many faces it seems to take on now a days. In order for this book to completely work for you it's a question we must visit.

What is success? We often measure our success based on our society and cultural standards. This mentality leaves us to keep up with the Joneses! This superficial artificial meaning of success often leaves us feeling barren and unfulfilled.

What if I told you that success is redefined and based on that individual, that no answer was really wrong- if that is how that individual defined success for themselves? If we all realized this we would live even more fulfilling lives.

So what is the actual definition you ask? Success is "the outcome, result, favorable or desired outcome, the correct or desired result of an attempt" according to Merriam -Webster online dictionary. This next one is my favorite because of its simplicity and profundity. It reads Success is the" accomplishment of an aim or purpose" according to the Google's online dictionary.

So what does this all mean? As long as you accomplish the goal or aim that you have set that is success! You don't have to have several cars and homes to be successful! You don't have to be rich to be successful. I'll reiterate *for one to be successful one must simply accomplish their goal.* Success doesn't come over night and there is no short cut to obtain it. After failing or missing the mark you must try again and again until that goal is accomplished.

Remember there is no elevator to success only stairs.
Most people we believe are successful overnight have put the effort and work in sometimes for many years before they receive their big opportunity and or break. They also go through many attempts that didn't land on their intended goal.

Take a moment before you begin this book to define what success is for you. Think of what success means for you in each area of your life and write it down. If it is obtaining wealth, cars and homes so be it, however I challenge you to really dig deep to find where the *"satisfying success"* lies for you.

Once I was able to define what success meant for me it freed me all the more to be intentional and focused. I realized for me that *"satisfying success"* meant walking in my purpose daily and this was also the foundation. Everything I desired stemmed from me being willing to walk in the fullness of that purpose. I am blessed to see the fruit of this in my life every day!

I reckon success is not just to accomplish the aim or goal but *true* *"satisfying success"* is the fulfillment of knowing you're in purpose and seeing that aim or goal contribute, influence, impact, inspire, bless, empower and give to others while it gives back to you as well.

Table of Contents

"Don't stress over the things you can't control, rather put your energy into the things you can."

-Robert Lee Robbins

Chapter 1
Locating, Seeing & Loving Self

"How can one improve if one is not aware of their current condition or state?"

-Robyn Robbins

Locating, Seeing & Loving Self

This human experience we call life, right? Oh, how I have been around the mountain quite a bit my friend and if you have this book you probably have to. Experiences have caused me to get to a place where self- reflection has become one of my best friends. Being able to look at myself has helped me to see myself and locate myself instead of passing the blame off on others. In doing this maturity has been inevitable and I have been able to readjust to go in the right direction that is best for my life.

Blaming others, even if they do have a hand in it gives away our personal power - giving others control over us. What would happen if you got to a place where you reflect on self instead and think on the things you can do different? It comes down to — what kind of woman or man you desire to be? We can't change others but we can change ourselves….. With the power of decision!

This may not be applicable to some but for me, I realized that I could not measure myself based on my own thoughts, but it was important to be able to really see myself to change the outcome. This is where my faith came in, my prayer became Lord, Jesus helps me to see me the way you see me. It was only then that my eyes were truly opened, and I was able to measure based on God's standards instead of my own. I saw His love for me, and I saw the things that were displeasing not only to Him but to myself as well. That experience caused me to come up higher if you will.

At the same time, I was reminded not only to locate and see myself or the reality of my current condition or state but to love myself through it. In other words, as you see the thing you would like to change don't badger or condemn yourself for it.

Understand that no one is perfect, dare to strive for wholeness NOT perfection. As you embark upon these "things" don't be afraid to call it like you see it. If it looks like a duck and it quacks like a duck, then call it a duck! Don't hinder or sabotage yourself by sugarcoating the things, persons, places and or relationships that are not good for you.

So as you go through this book be honest with yourself, forgive, love and commit to doing the work. You will be glad you did!!

Sincerely, Robyn

DAY 1

"Who are You?"

(Week 1 Monday)

We are always evolving and most of the time we forget to spend time with self in a way where we are able to reevaluate and locate self. We find ourselves in places we would have never imagined because we didn't take the time to define our standards. Have you ever heard the saying "If you stand for nothing, you'll fall for anything"?

Well, it's true, in the past I have found myself in compromising situations where I ultimately compromised for whatever reasons (whether it was to be accepted, liked, to fit in etc.). I realized that I wasn't clear on all of the things I stood for and why I stood for them. I was prompted to make a list and in doing so I was able to see how and why I easily fell and failed in certain areas.... I wasn't sure of whom I was so I didn't have a stance and the inevitable happened - I fell for anything.

This exercise prompts you to dig deep and will assist in seeing what things are the same and what things have changed.
 It helps us to remember what's important in life. As life goes on, we change, we grow. Write a list of likes and dislikes, a list of your goals and dreams, a list of what you stand for, a list of things that you want to work on pertaining to self. Most importantly don't forget to answer the question "Who are you?"

"Character cannot be developed in ease and quiet. Only through experience of trial and suffering can the soul be strengthened, ambition inspired, and success achieved."
-Helen Keller

Challenge # 1: Who are you? What are your likes, dislikes, goals, dreams, make a list of what you stand for and a list of things you would like to work on throughout this time.

_____

_____

_____

_____

_____

_____

_____

_____

_____

_____

_____

_____

_____

_____

_____

_____

_____

_____

_____

_____

_____

_____

_____

_____

_____

_____

_____

_____

_____

_____

_____

_____

_____

_____

Journal

What are your thoughts?

How are you feeling?

_____
_____
_____
_____
_____
_____
_____
_____
_____
_____
_____
_____
_____
_____
_____
_____
_____
_____
_____
_____
_____
_____
_____
_____
_____
_____
_____
_____
_____
_____

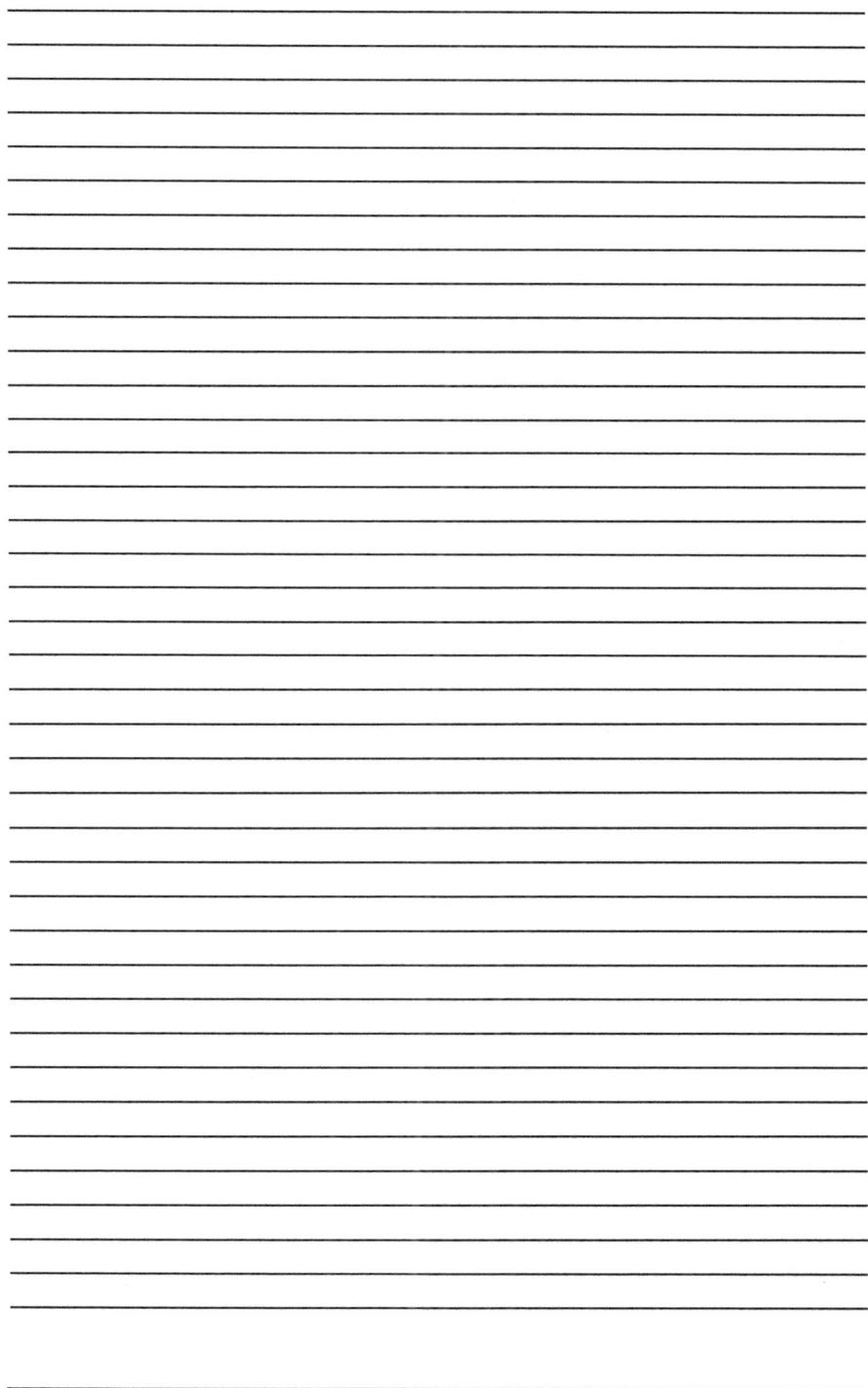

DAY 2

"No Clutter!"

(Week 1 Tuesday)

Now that we have reminded ourselves of who we are and where we are at with self it's time to do away with the clutter! Whatever doesn't and didn't line up with who you are or want to be and where you want to go in life MUST GO! Now this in itself will be a process but commit to it. Don't be afraid to shed people, unhealthy relationships, unhealthy environments, things and or habits. Assess and do daily until the process is complete.

"Keeping baggage from the past will leave no room for the happiness in the future"
-Wayne L. Misner

Challenge #2: What are the things that must go and why?

Journal

What are your thoughts?

How are you feeling?

_____
_____
_____
_____
_____
_____
_____
_____
_____
_____
_____
_____
_____
_____
_____
_____
_____
_____
_____
_____
_____
_____
_____
_____
_____
_____
_____
_____
_____

DAY 3

"A Day of Refining"

(Week 1 Wednesday)

Being rough around the edges isn't a bad thing but what happens when our edges are sharp, cutting ourselves as well as others? It is important to be careful what we take in from others however what happens when you begin to hear the same things over and over again! Is it possible that there may be some truth to it? What are the things that have been harmful to you and the ones you love? Let's Examine....

"A self-absorbed person can only see the faults of others but they are colorblind to their own"
-Unknown

Challenge #3: What are the things others mention to you most that they believe are negative?

Journal

What are your thoughts?

How are you feeling?

_____

_____

_____

_____

_____

_____

_____

_____

_____

_____

_____

_____

_____

_____

_____

_____

_____

_____

_____

_____

_____

_____

_____

_____

_____

_____

_____

_____

_____

_____

DAY 4

"Having Patience while in Pursuit"

(Week 1 Thursday)

Sometimes we want things to happen fast, so fast that it would manifest overnight! Remember to have patience with yourself and trust the process that you are in and will be in. Refocusing takes work and consistent application.

Today write down 3 things you would like to have accomplished by the end of this 40 day challenge then write down how you will accomplish these 3 goals.

"All our dreams can come true if we have the courage to pursue them."
-Walt Disney

Challenge #4: List 3 things you want to accomplish, what is needed to accomplish them and how you will accomplish these goals? Be sure to identify a support system if needed.

1._____

_____
_____
_____
_____
_____
_____
_____
_____
_____
_____

2._____

_____
_____
_____
_____
_____
_____
_____
_____
_____

3._____

_____
_____
_____
_____
_____
_____
_____
_____
_____
_____
_____
_____
_____
_____

Journal

What are your thoughts?

How are you feeling

_____
_____
_____
_____
_____
_____
_____
_____
_____
_____
_____
_____
_____
_____
_____
_____
_____
_____
_____
_____
_____
_____
_____
_____
_____
_____
_____
_____
_____

DAY 5

"Time of Reflection"

(Week 1 Friday)

The Time of reflection begins on Friday and ends on Sunday. Take this time to complete the challenges you may have missed and reflect on self. Begin to visualize the changes that you want to see and the goals you want to accomplish. Below you may journal your thoughts feelings and or plan to execute these things throughout this time of reflection.

"Only by much searching and mining are gold and diamonds obtained, and man can find every truth connected with his being if he will dig deep into the mine of his soul."
-James Allen

Challenge #5: Being completely honest and vulnerable with self, what would you say your current state or condition is? Search and dig deep within....

DAY 8

"What does your Advertisement Say?"
(Week 2 Monday)

If your life was presently a constant advertisement campaign available
for ALL to see, what would we see? What would the message be? This
one can be a doozie but this is why we are here in this time and in this
space. We must be committed to being honest, vulnerable and doing
the work that needs to be done. If you are not satisfied with those
answers- then there is work to be done! You are not alone, now shake
loose and let's make it happen!

"It all comes down to the kind of woman or man you want to be"
-Renee Jones

Challenge #8: Write the answers below to the following questions-
What would we see, what would the message be? What would you like
to see? What message would you like to convey?

___

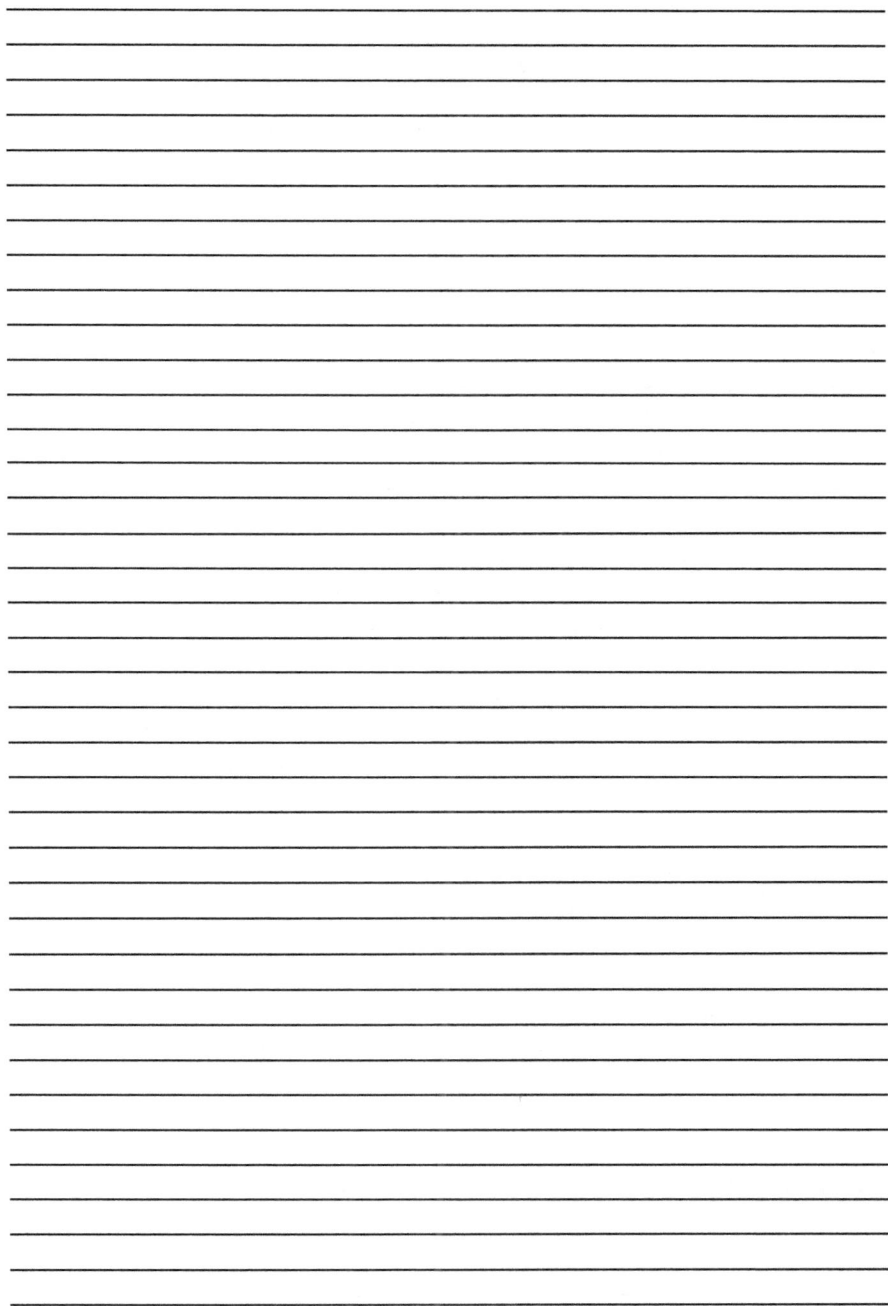

Journal

What are your thoughts?

How are you feeling?

_____
_____
_____
_____
_____
_____
_____
_____
_____
_____
_____
_____
_____
_____
_____
_____
_____
_____
_____
_____
_____
_____
_____
_____
_____
_____
_____

DAY 9

"LOVE ON YOU!"
(Week 2 Tuesday)

This has been a ride thus far, we have been digging deep, completely vulnerable and committed to doing the work. Don't forget about ALL the great qualities and characteristics you have! Look in the mirror and create affirmations of love and endearment. Do this daily and as often as you like! Love on you!!!! At this point of the challenge we have been shedding a lot of unwanted things, habits, people and environments. This could be very taxing emotionally, mentally, physically and spiritually. Revitalize by speaking over yourself, treat yourself to the spa, meditate or do something that you like that will energize and revitalize your being.

"I am overflowing with joy, vitality and energy -- I'm unstoppable!" – Dr. Carmen Harra

"I am loved, loveable, imperfectly perfect embracing ALL of me"
– Robyn Robbins

Challenge # 9: Create affirmations for yourself, 2 affirmations of love, encouragement and endearment each. Post a copy of these affirmations on your bathroom mirror and say daily!

_____
_____
_____
_____
_____
_____
_____
_____
_____
_____
_____
_____
_____
_____
_____
_____
_____
_____
_____
_____
_____
_____
_____
_____
_____
_____
_____
_____

Journal

What are your thoughts?

How are you feeling

_____
_____
_____
_____
_____
_____
_____
_____
_____
_____
_____
_____
_____
_____
_____
_____
_____
_____
_____
_____
_____
_____
_____
_____
_____
_____
_____
_____
_____

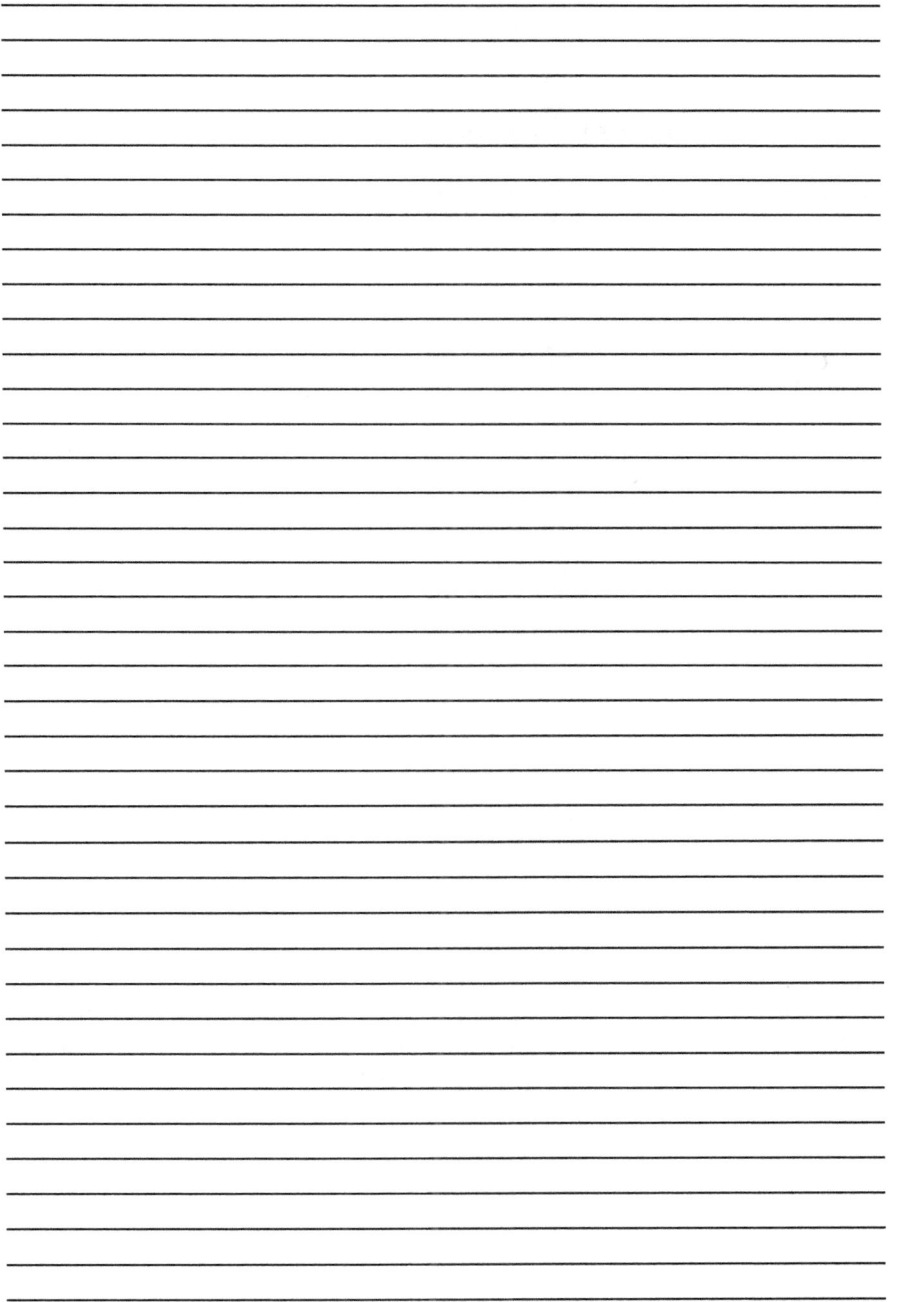

DAY 10

"Finish What You Started!"
(Week 2 Wednesday)

What dreams, goals, or ideas did you start and for whatever reason it fell along the wayside? What tasks in your life are incomplete? Today take inventory and make a list of these things only.

Next to it write the reason why it's incomplete. Then make a second list with the things you still desire to complete from the first list. Be specific on how you will complete each goal or task and the time frame each one will take to complete it.

You can do it!! (Only list the things you are really passionate and or serious about.) At this time you should begin to see a reoccurring theme in your dreams and or goals, take special note to that.

"Faith is an interactive word that thrives off of action, so yes believe you can do it but also take action that demonstrates your belief. Remember it doesn't matter if no one else believes in your dreams or goals, you must believe! The best answer to their unbelief is the manifestation or reality of your dream and or goal"
-Robyn Robbins

Challenge # 10: Follow the directions above and write your answers to the questions above, below.

_____
_____
_____
_____
_____
_____
_____
_____
_____
_____
_____
_____
_____
_____
_____
_____
_____
_____
_____
_____
_____
_____
_____
_____
_____
_____
_____
_____
_____
_____
_____
_____
_____
_____

Journal

What are your thoughts?

How are you feeling?

_____
_____
_____
_____
_____
_____
_____
_____
_____
_____
_____
_____
_____
_____
_____
_____
_____
_____
_____
_____
_____
_____
_____
_____
_____
_____
_____
_____
_____
_____

DAY 11

"To Thine own Self be True!"
(Week 2 Thursday)

Whatever you strive to do or be in this life, let it come from the place of truth. Don't worry about people! People will always have an opinion. Walking in and with integrity may be a hard thing to do but it starts with being honest with self First!

Congratulations these last 2 weeks you have been facing, reevaluating self and getting self in order. One of the hardest things to do at times! I commend you for not sabotaging yourself by getting in your own way! Congratulations again!!

"I prefer to be true to myself, even at the hazard of incurring the ridicule of others, rather than to be false, and to incur my own abhorrence."
-Frederick Douglass.

Challenge # 11: What have you not been true to when it comes to self? What have you hidden?

Journal

What are your thoughts?

How are you feeling?

_____
_____
_____
_____
_____
_____
_____
_____
_____
_____
_____
_____
_____
_____
_____
_____
_____
_____
_____
_____
_____
_____
_____
_____
_____
_____
_____
_____
_____

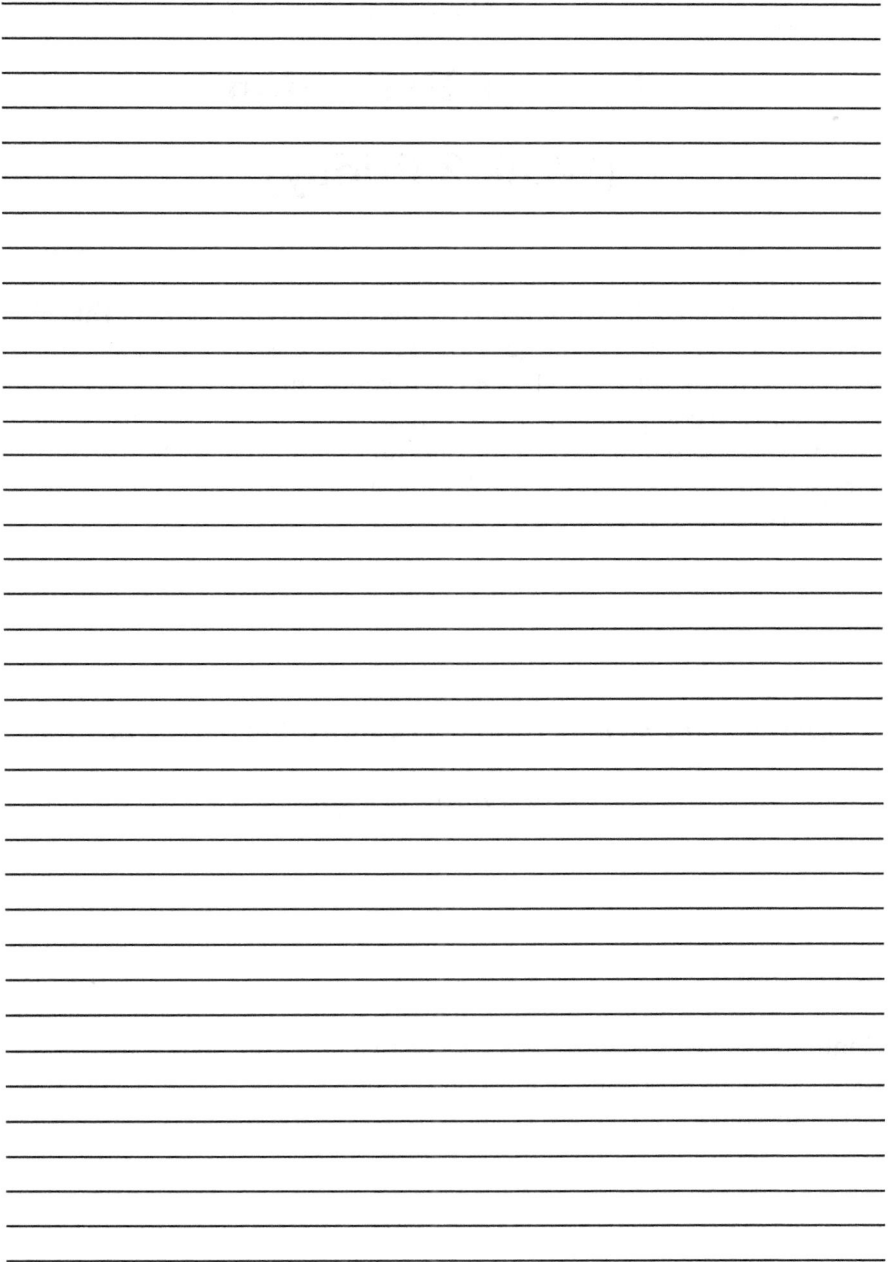

DAY 12

"Time of Reflection"

(Week 2 Friday)

The Time of reflection begins on Friday and ends on Sunday. Take this time to complete the challenges you may have missed and reflect on self. Begin to visualize the changes that you want to see and the goals you want to accomplish. Below you may journal your thoughts feelings over the weekend and throughout this time of reflection. You are almost there, 4 more weeks to go! Are you closer to your goals, to the new you?

"Life can only be understood backwards; but it must be lived forwards."
— Søren Kierkegaard

Challenge #12: Visualize the changes that you want to see and the goals you want to accomplish every morning before you get out of the bed. Journal your time of Reflection

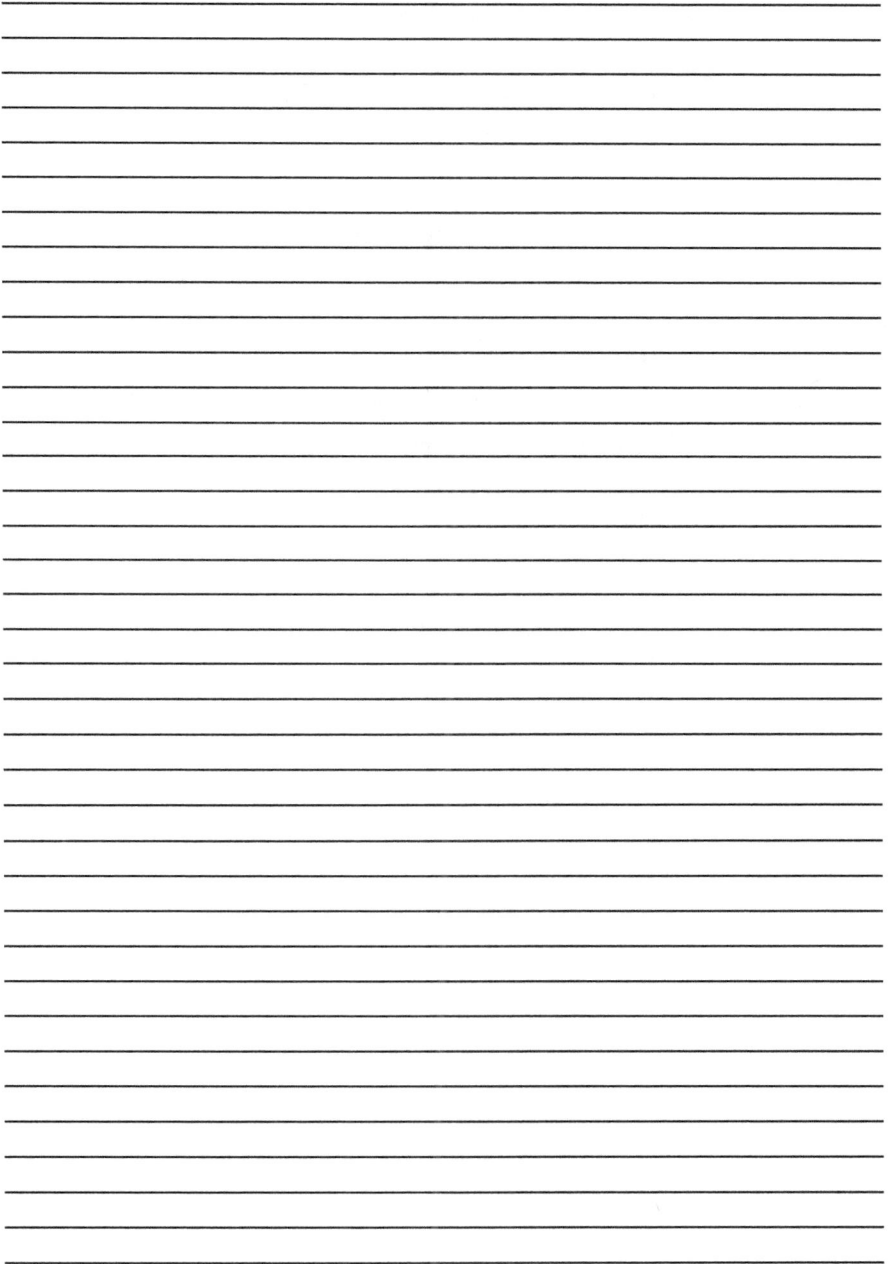

Chapter 2

The Mind & Mentality

"The mind contributes greatly to our daily outcome but your mentality shapes and creates your world. Never underestimate the Power of thought!"

-Robyn Robbins

The Mind & Mentality

The mind is a powerful thing and one of our greatest assets! The mind and mentality contribute greatly to our perspectives, actions, mood, and the manner in which one carries themselves among other things. What if we intentionally used the mind to produce positive productive results thus transforming the immediate world around us? How you ask? Through decision making- choose the thought that's best.

For example, one could either see the glass half empty or half full- choose the one that produces positive thinking and run with it! We can either see a mistake in business as a downfall, a loss or as a learning curve- I reiterate choose the one that produces positive thinking and run with it! You will notice that positive tangible results soon begin to follow this positive thinking. The repetition of this application begins to condition your mind to think on a specific frequency thus producing positive results natural once used to being applied.

For example: I worked as a C.N.A and in my early days there were some clients that were rather difficult. There were times when I would take it personal and want to give up. I couldn't understand why they couldn't see I was only there to help.

I would share with my friend the distress I had been experiencing and she told me if you change your perspective and react in a positive manner you could change that work environment. True to my nature I tested what she explained to me and my findings were remarkable. I would say to myself on my way to work" it's not personal, they are just settled in their ways, and instead of being offended I choose to shower them with love and kindness." Do you know that that decision to choose the positive thought and action gave me the most pleasant work atmosphere ever!?

So much so that my client would scold her husband if she felt he was being harsh. She would say "Don't you talk to my Robyn that way," she'd warn. This experience opened my eyes and showed me that we really can create or affect the immediate world around us.

Even in the bible we are urged to be renewed in our minds (Romans 12:2). It is important that the mind goes through a transformation. The revelation I received was this: the old negative mind filled with old negative thought patterns and old negative habits equals negative distorted perception and perspective, but a renewed mind filled with new understanding, new thought patterns and new positive habits equals fresh positive perception and perspective thus giving clear sight and positive results.

DAY 15

"Perspective!"

(Week 3 Monday)

If it's true that our eyes are the windows to our souls, then we must be careful of what we allow our eyes to take in! What we take in either creates shapes or changes our appetites. If we want positivity in our lives, careers, and businesses then we must feed ourselves positive images, positive conversations and entertain positive thoughts to create the outcome we desire!

"We can complain because rose bushes have thorns, or rejoice because thorn bushes have roses."
— Abraham Lincoln

Challenge #15: Are you guarding what you hear, see and speak? How is your perspective?

Journal

What are your thoughts?

How are you feeling?

_____
_____
_____
_____
_____
_____
_____
_____
_____
_____
_____
_____
_____
_____
_____
_____
_____
_____
_____
_____
_____
_____
_____
_____
_____
_____
_____
_____
_____
_____
_____
_____
_____
_____

DAY 16

"Can you're Focus be affected by what you Eat?"

(Week 3 Tuesday)

Studies have shown that there is a lot of truth to this! Have you ever ate and felt sleepy afterwards or noticed you have more energy after consuming certain foods? Today evaluate your diet and be sure to pack it with super foods. Remember better eating = a better focused you!

Make changes that will fit your lifestyle, not temporary changes for a moment or the purposes of this challenge. Really dig deep and make changes you are committed to keep for a lifetime! Below you will find a short list of foods that give energy and help improve focus.

Super foods: Brain Power. Focus. Energy. Mood

Salmon (improves performance and alertness)
Green Tea (a great alternative to coffee if you don't like it and is loaded with antioxidants and helps to enhance your mood)
Avocado (improves concentration and helps lower cholesterol)
Berries (dark berries, blueberries, raspberries and blackberries helps to keep you energized and assist in avoiding dips or crashing)
Veggies (cabbage, kale, cauliflower and Brussels sprouts help you to avoid a blood sugar crash)

Dark Chocolate, Spinach, Carrots, Beets, Walnuts, Coffee and Olive oil are all great stimulants for the Brain as well as the others…Can You say Brain Power!!! Oats, Quinoa, Turkey, and Almonds are also great Super foods to have in our diet. Please consult with your doctor before changing your diet.

Challenge #16: Purchase the super foods you like and look up recipes that best fit you. Document how you feel after changing up your diet and consuming more water after 1 week….How is your energy, how is your focus?

_____

_____

_____

_____

_____

_____

_____

_____

_____

_____

_____

_____

_____

_____

_____

_____

_____

_____

_____

_____

_____

_____

_____

_____

_____

_____

_____

_____

_____

_____

_____

_____

_____

Journal

What are your thoughts?

How are you feeling?

DAY 17

"Are you a worker bee or a Queen/"King" Bee?"

(Week 3 Wednesday)

In order to produce success, there is something one needs besides tenacity and resilience. It's the mentality of success. The mind or mindset controls or contributes to our outcome. This is why it is vital to groom yourself with the proper mentality as it will serve as a great foundation for you.

This mentality becomes a way of being and it influences the decisions you will make going forward. What's the difference between the worker bee and the queen bee? Or why do ants thrive? The assignment is to study one of the two and document your findings!! If you are feeling ambitious do both. You will be glad you did!

"Great works are performed, not by strength, but by perseverance." - Samuel Johnson

Challenge # 17:   What's the difference between the worker bee and the queen bee? Why do ants thrive? Make note of the characteristics and function of the worker bee and the queen bee. Study the way they work, build, live, and interact. Be sure to notate how these things can apply to you.

Journal

What are your thoughts?

How are you feeling?

_____
_____
_____
_____
_____
_____
_____
_____
_____
_____
_____
_____
_____
_____
_____
_____
_____
_____
_____
_____
_____
_____
_____
_____
_____
_____
_____
_____
_____
_____
_____
_____
_____

DAY 18

"Practice = Consistency"

(Week 3 Thursday)

If we make the effort to apply the practices we have learned daily the result will be consistency! As we do this the muscle called "discipline" is being strengthened! If we commit to doing this the outcome in our businesses, careers, spiritual walk and lives would be phenomenal! Have you exercised your muscles today? Where are you not yet consistent?

"Daily Practice begot Consistency, Consistency begot discipline thus birthing and building Character "   -Robyn Robbins

Challenge #18: Where are you not yet consistent, which area or part of your life lacks consistency? How are you going to become consistent in this/these areas?

Journal

What are your thoughts?

How are you feeling?

_____
_____
_____
_____
_____
_____
_____
_____
_____
_____
_____
_____
_____
_____
_____
_____
_____
_____
_____
_____
_____
_____
_____
_____
_____
_____
_____
_____
_____
_____
_____

DAY 19

"Time of Reflection"

(Week 3 Friday)

The Time of reflection begins on Friday and ends on Sunday. Take this time to complete the challenges you may have missed and reflect on self. Begin to visualize the changes that you want to see and the goals you want to accomplish.

Below you may journal your thoughts feelings over the weekend and throughout this time of reflection. You are almost there, 3 more weeks to go! Are you closer to your goals, to the new you? Are you grateful for the things you have and the accomplishments you have made?

"Gratitude unlocks the fullness of life. It turns what we have into enough, and more. It turns denial into acceptance, chaos to order, confusion to clarity. It can turn a meal into a feast, a house into a home, a stranger into a friend. Gratitude makes sense of our past, brings peace for today and creates a vision for tomorrow."
— Melody Beattie

Challenge #19: Continue to visualize the changes that you want to see and the goals you want to accomplish and give Thanks for everything you have every morning before you get out of the bed. Journal your time of Reflection.

Chapter 3

You're Environments

"Our surroundings can give positive contributions or negative contributions. It's up to you to decide which one you accept and allow."

-Robyn Robbins

You're Environments

Our Environment plays a major role in our lives. It can even affect our mental and emotional health as well. According to the study that was done at Princeton University, they tested the amount of stimuli a person was exposed to concluding that clutter directly and negatively affects our focus. I believe if we can be affected by physical clutter it is more than possible that emotional clutter and mental clutter can also affect our focus negatively as well.

Our environments can stimulate us positively or aggravate and irritate us for the negative. Now I'm not saying that you'll never encounter these types of environments, I'm saying that you have the power to create the environment you want by the decisions you make by simply choosing and sticking to what works for you. Don't be afraid to dismiss whatever is in your environment that is hindering you or interfering with your focus.

It is important with this to have a balance. Why you ask? Sometimes certain things or persons enter our environment to foster growth within us although at times it can be so uncomfortable and even stressful. If we get rid of every little thing that works against us we won't ever evolve. So do use fair judgment on when and what to remove and when to allow a person or thing to remove itself.

For example the room I work in was out of order and a bit to cluttered for my liking so I rearranged some things, through away some things, and organized some things until everything was in sync, in order. I even added a touch of personality by painting an accent wall.

Example #2: As I continued on my journey for a better more productive me. Everyone wasn't genuinely happy for me. Some people came in the form of friend when the whole time they were looking to distract and destroy what I was trying to build due to them being unhappy with self. When I realized I went from no drama to being in drama just because of my association with them it was clear I had to break ties and never allow them in my personal space again.

So you're getting my drift here. Use the best judgment possible and don't be afraid to consult a wise friend or associate for wisdom when you are unsure. This friend can be a therapist, coach, pastor counselor etc.

DAY 22

"Prioritizing & Time Management"

(Week 4 Monday)

Life can be a lot, especially when you juggle more than 2 hats! Sometimes we don't realize what we can do without. Today let's get rid of the clutter in our time and schedules, only leaving room for what's really important, truly matters and fits the new you that's emerging. This is one of the keys to balance and success.

This task can be difficult if we are not willing to see that are time is truly valuable. It's important to have a healthy balance- having time for family, work, your relationships, fun/recreation and what we call "Me Time" (time with self). Each is equally important and adds value to us. During this time of the challenge I felt led to even take it a step further and rid myself of the clutter in my immediate space. I rearranged my home to fit this new mindset I was embracing.

I then cleaned out my closets and donated the things I wasn't using. I didn't realize it then but I have come to realize that this was an outward expression of the *ORDER* my life was embracing. We had bought all types of things that help to organize our closet space and counter space. When we were done everything had a place and what no longer had a place was given away! As we grow we can't take everything with us- we outgrow certain things and its okay to let them go....whatever you're *"them"* maybe!

"You can't make up for lost time. You can only do better in the future."
— Ashley Ormon

Challenge #22: Review your daily schedules and modify them to fit the You Now, Not the You Then. Get rid of the clutter in your immediate space (chose 1 room) whether it's a closet, office and or bedroom; adjust your space to fit YOU!

_____
_____
_____
_____
_____
_____
_____
_____
_____
_____
_____
_____
_____
_____
_____
_____
_____
_____
_____
_____
_____
_____
_____
_____
_____
_____
_____
_____
_____
_____
_____
_____
_____

Journal

What are your thoughts?

How are you feeling?

_____

_____

_____

_____

_____

_____

_____

_____

_____

_____

_____

_____

_____

_____

_____

_____

_____

_____

_____

_____

_____

_____

_____

_____

_____

_____

_____

_____

_____

_____

DAY 23

"Prioritizing & Time Management" Part 2

(Week 4 Tuesday)

Now that we have gotten rid of the clutter in our immediate space and the clutter from our schedules we can see more easily what can be done once a week, every 2 weeks and or daily. Try to make the start of your day "Top Heavy" with the things of most importance, urgency and or the tasks that require the most efforts then allow the things that you can do easily to follow after.

In addition create a deadline for each task. It's hard to get things accomplish when there is nothing holding or no one holding us accountable. By giving a deadline we create our own accountability support system. This will help strengthen the muscle we call discipline. You will begin to see just how productive and balanced you are becoming!

"The key is not to prioritize what's on your schedule, but to schedule your priorities." -Stephen Covey

"The bad news is time flies. The good news is you're the pilot." — Michael Altshuler

Challenge #23: Recreate your schedule allocating deadlines and how often something is to be done. Don't forget to keep your schedule balanced and remember your time is valuable so don't waste it on things that don't really matter to you. Note- Make your daily schedule Top Heavy.

Journal

What are your thoughts?

How are you feeling?

DAY 24

"Distractions"
(Week 4 Wednesday)

Around this time of the challenge you will notice that distractions will try to find its way in if it hasn't already to try and hinder or even stop this process and or journey. At those times remember the outcome you are striving for!

This is where your fight comes in; stay focused and remember it's worth it in the end! To help combat this start your day with prayer, meditation, visualization or a combination that works best for you!!! Apply Daily!!!

"One way to boost our will power and focus is to manage our distractions instead of letting them manage us." *-Daniel Goleman*

Challenge #24: What distractions have you been experiencing and how do you plan to manage them?

Journal

What are your thoughts?

How are you feeling?

_____
_____
_____
_____
_____
_____
_____
_____
_____
_____
_____
_____
_____
_____
_____
_____
_____
_____
_____
_____
_____
_____
_____
_____
_____
_____
_____
_____
_____

DAY 25

"Time of Reflection"

(Week 4 Friday)

The Time of reflection begins on Friday and ends on Sunday. Take this time to complete the challenges you may have missed and reflect on self. Begin to visualize the changes that you want to see and the goals you want to accomplish. Below you may journal your thoughts feelings over the weekend and throughout this time of reflection. You are almost there, 2 more weeks to go! Are you closer to your goals, to the new you? Are you grateful for the things you have and the accomplishments you have made?

"Gratitude unlocks the fullness of life. It turns what we have into enough, and more. It turns denial into acceptance, chaos to order, confusion to clarity. It can turn a meal into a feast, a house into a home, a stranger into a friend. Gratitude makes sense of our past, brings peace for today and creates a vision for tomorrow."— Melody Beattie

Challenge #25: Continue to visualize the changes that you want to see and the goals you want to accomplish and give Thanks for everything you have every morning before you get out of the bed. Journal your time of Reflection

Chapter 4

The New You Emerging!

"Being intentional daily, willing to do the work, upholding your values, standards, beliefs and never giving up are a few ingredients needed in order to see the you that you desire!"

-Robyn Robbins

The New You Emerging!

This is when all the hard work yields results and you begin to notice all the different things you've worked on and for manifesting! You're excited by the progress you've made and it feels pretty darn good!

Remember that consistency is key and to remain successful one needs to avoid picking back up unhealthy habits, environments, relationships and old mind sets. Allow all that you have learned to be applied over and over again.

Remember taking care of self is a major key for you. If your health diminishes- what good are you to yourself, family, friends, business, and or relationships and so on? Try to eat as healthy as you possibly can and exercise weekly as it helps to give you energy. Manage your time and balance the hats you wear as best as you can. Remember to be patient and to love on self as much as you can!

This New You looks good on you my friend!!!

DAY 28

"Sowing Only What You Desire To Reap"

(Week 5 Monday)

Today begin to practice releasing only what you want to receive! This can be a hard thing, especially when the situation and or person make it such. I sometimes still struggle with this but I have to remember not to indulge those feelings of anger or even revenge and understand hurting people hurt people.

Instead I try to think no one is perfect and put myself in their shoes all while trying to embrace the thought of how would I want to be treated in this situation. In these moments try to think....what would I like to receive? How would I like to be treated?

"Don't judge each day by the harvest you reap but by the seeds that you plant."   *-Robert Louis Stevenson*

Challenge #28:   How do you want to be treated, really define what this looks like?

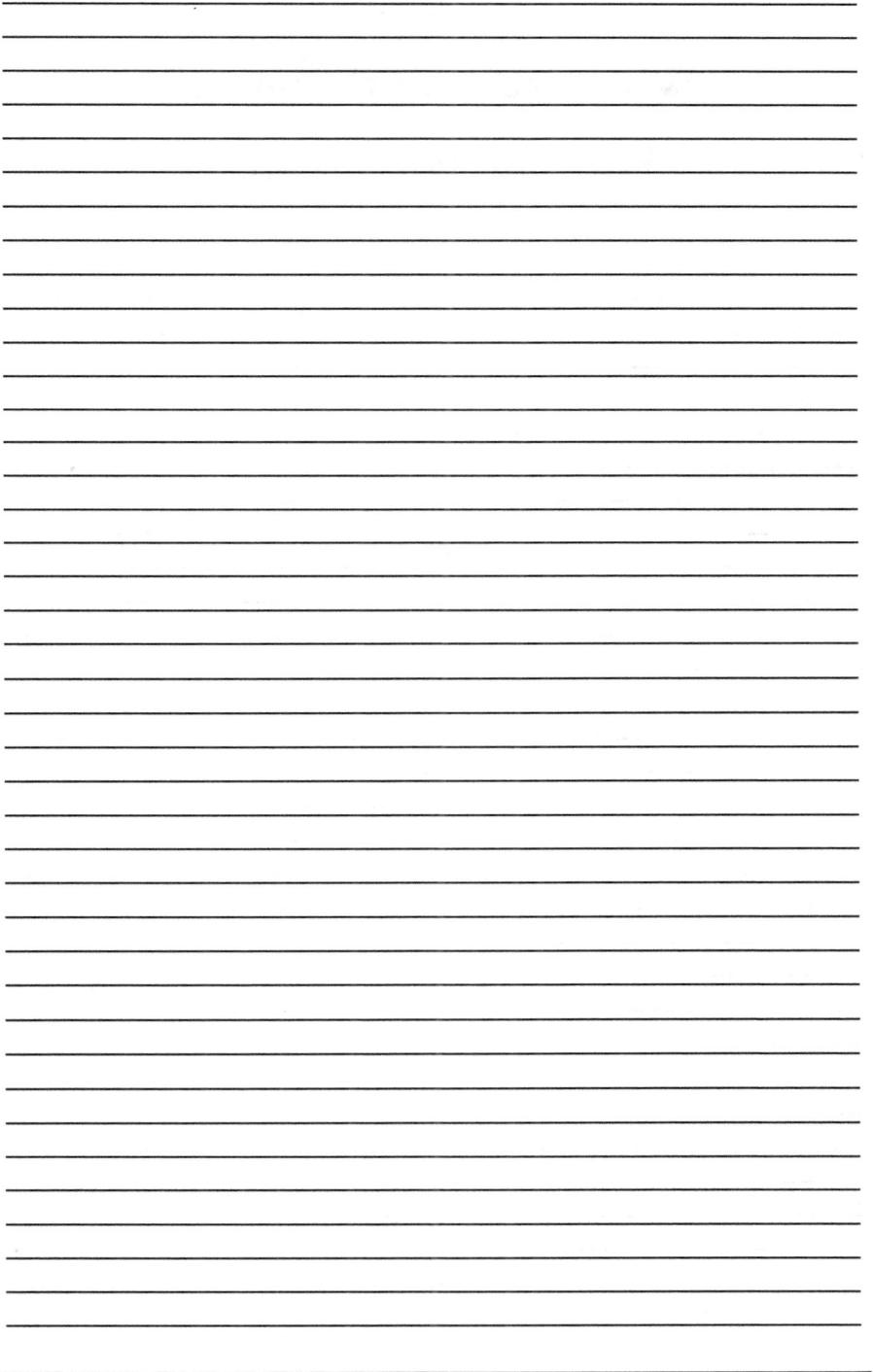

Journal

What are your thoughts?

How are you feeling?

DAY 29

"Necessary Adaptability"

(Week 5 Tuesday)

Sometimes we will experience the need to adjust as we go along. This can sometimes be vital to our success! How do you handle change? Can you make it work or do you freeze up? Today take a look at your adaptability radar.

"It is not the strongest or the most intelligent who will survive but those who can best manage change."
— Leon C. Megginson

Challenge #29: How do you handle change? Is there anything you would like to do different when handling change?

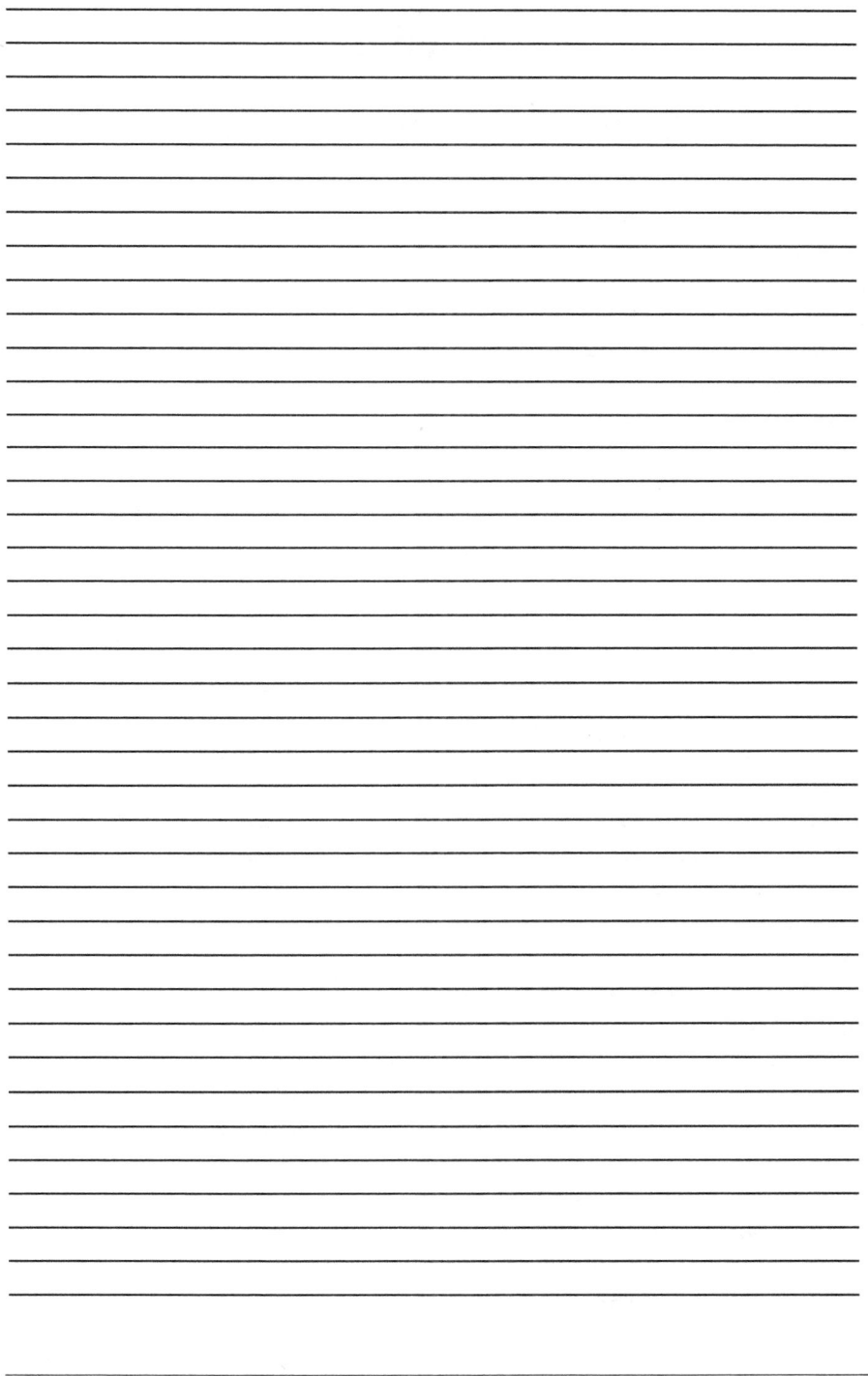

Journal

What are your thoughts?

How are you feeling?

_____
_____
_____
_____
_____
_____
_____
_____
_____
_____
_____
_____
_____
_____
_____
_____
_____
_____
_____
_____
_____
_____
_____
_____
_____
_____
_____
_____
_____
_____

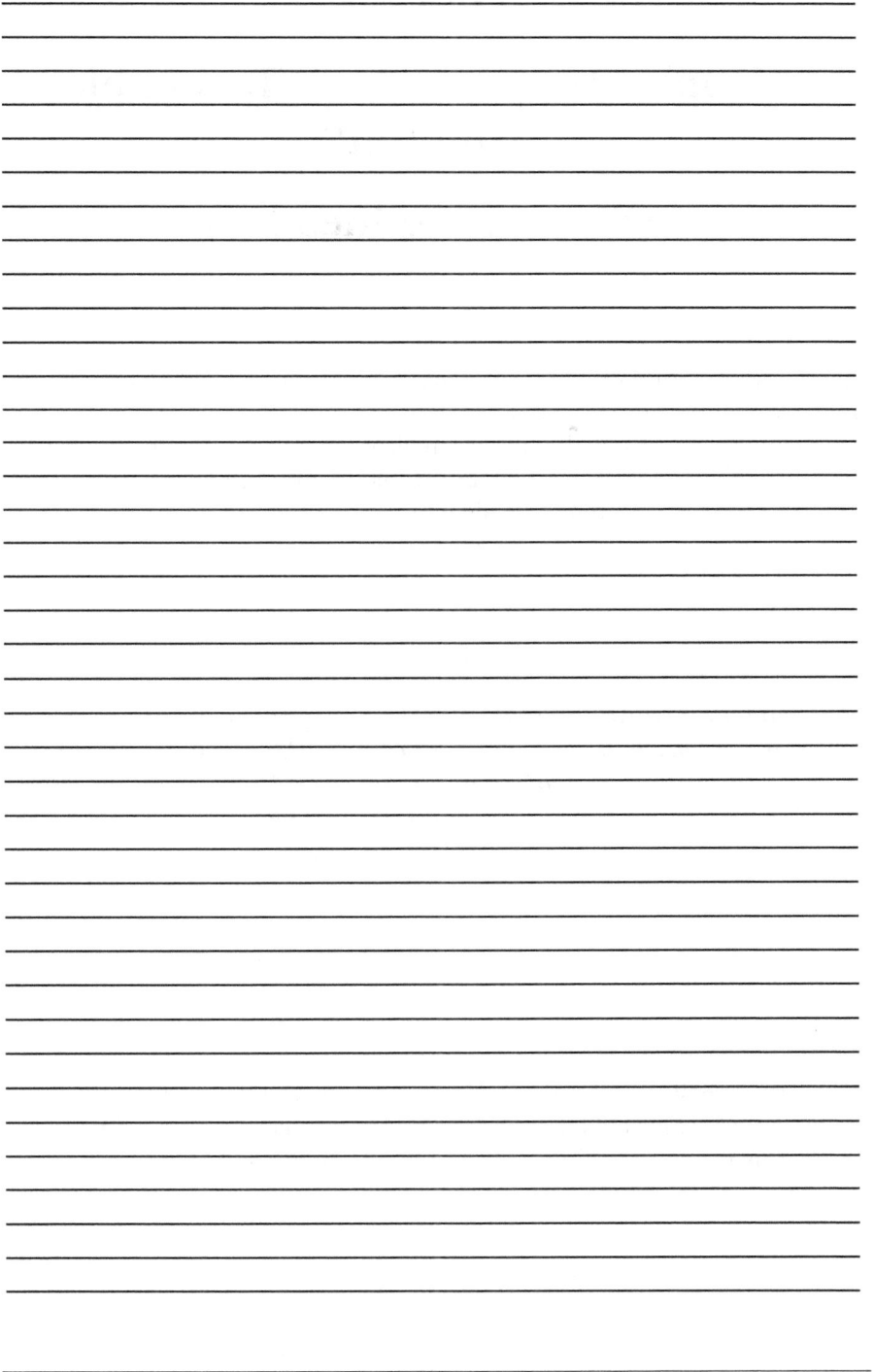

DAY 30

"Don't Miss Out On A Teachable Moment"

(Week 5 Wednesday)

Depending on one's perspective, the definition of a teachable moment may vary. However they are necessary to one's continued growth! Our teachable moment may be big or small. Whatever it is we must gleam from it and apply it. We are never too old or intelligent to receive correction and wisdom especially when it will further our lives in positive ways!

"A teachable spirit and a humbleness to admit your ignorance or your mistake will save you a lot of pain. However, if you're a person who knows it all, then you've got a lot of heavy-hearted experiences coming your way."
— Ron Carpenter Jr.

Challenge #30: What is one unforgettable teachable moment that you have had in the past? What teachable moment have you had since doing this refocus training and what have you learned from it?

Journal

What are your thoughts?

How are you feeling?

DAY 31

"Giving Up Is not an Option"
(Week 5 Thursday)

You are so close that you can see the finish line and taste the victory! You're scenery has changed, the people have changed, your conversations and thoughts have even changed. If you are experiencing a form of discomfort and isolation at this point you are right on track and on schedule.

It's like this process stripes you and starts you over in seed form. When a seed is in the ground it's in the dark and often alone. As that seed grows and began to rise above the ground it receives light but I imagine if that seed could feel as we feel ,discomfort is inevitable as it's growing parts breaks its way through parts of the seed (shell).

That's when the pains of true growth begin to announce it's self. The pain increases causing much discomfort and all of sudden thoughts to give up seem to be the best thing to do to alleviate the pain. In those moments remember the most intense pains come prior to the actual birth! You are in labor and birthing greatness and success is never easy.

"Most of the important things in the world have been accomplished by people who have kept on trying when there seemed to be no hope at all."
– Dale Carnegie

Challenge #31: What discomforts are you feeling at this point and how do you plan to overcome them?

_____
_____
_____
_____
_____
_____
_____
_____
_____
_____
_____
_____
_____
_____
_____
_____
_____
_____
_____
_____
_____
_____
_____
_____
_____
_____
_____
_____
_____
_____
_____
_____
_____
_____

Journal

What are your thoughts?

How are you feeling?

_____
_____
_____
_____
_____
_____
_____
_____
_____
_____
_____
_____
_____
_____
_____
_____
_____
_____
_____
_____
_____
_____
_____
_____
_____
_____
_____
_____
_____

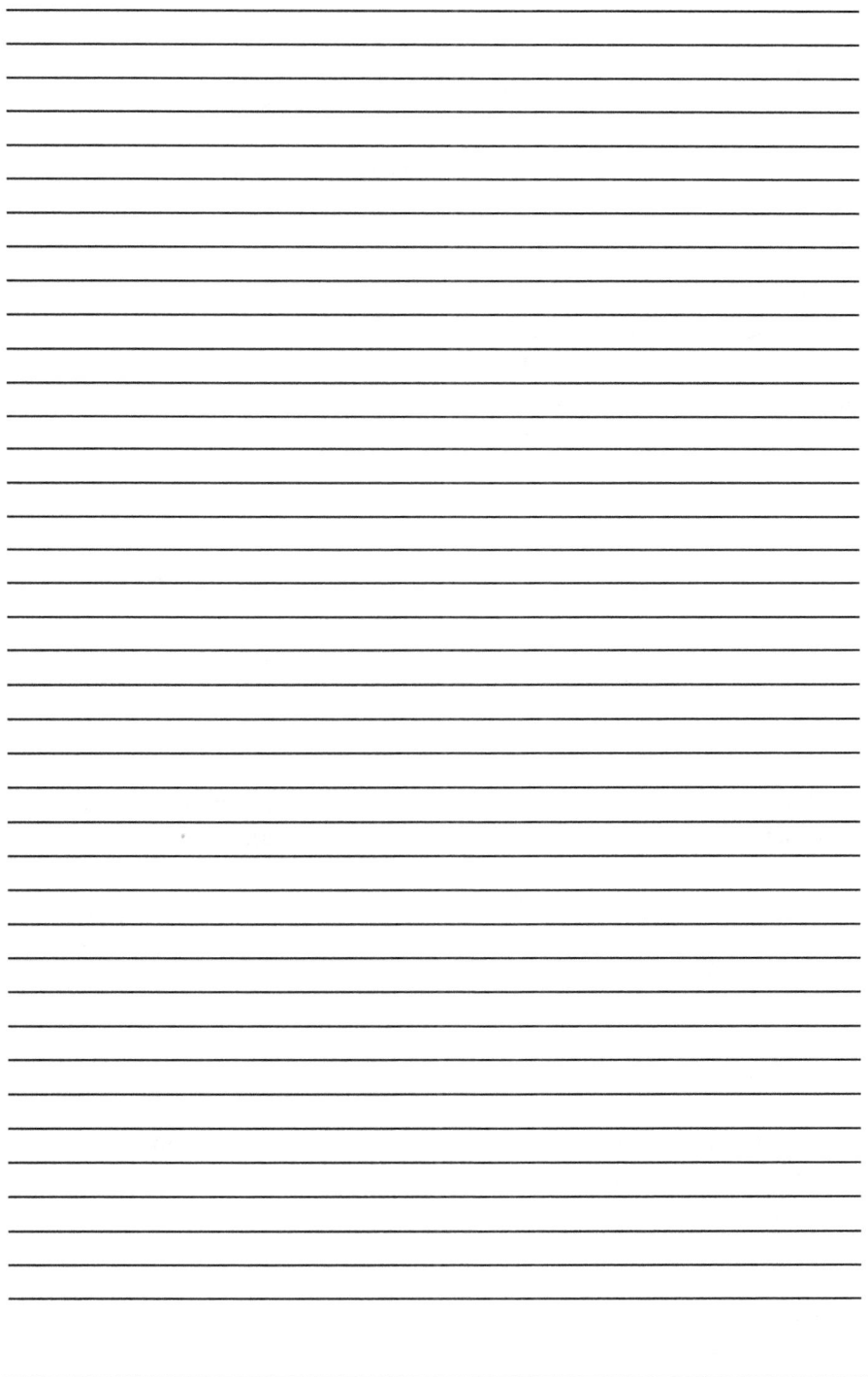

DAY 32

"Time of Reflection"

(Week 5 Friday)

The Time of reflection begins on Friday and ends on Sunday. Take this time to complete the challenges you may have missed and reflect on self. Begin to visualize the changes that you want to see and the goals you want to accomplish. Below you may journal your thoughts feelings over the weekend and throughout this time of reflection. You are almost there, 1 more week to go! Are you closer to your goals, to the new you? Are you grateful for the things you have and the accomplishments you have made?

"Reflect upon your present blessings -- of which every man has many -- not on your past misfortunes, of which all men have some."
— Charles Dickens

Challenge #32: Continue to visualize the changes that you want to see and the goals you want to accomplish and give Thanks for everything you have every morning before you get out of the bed. Journal your time of Reflection

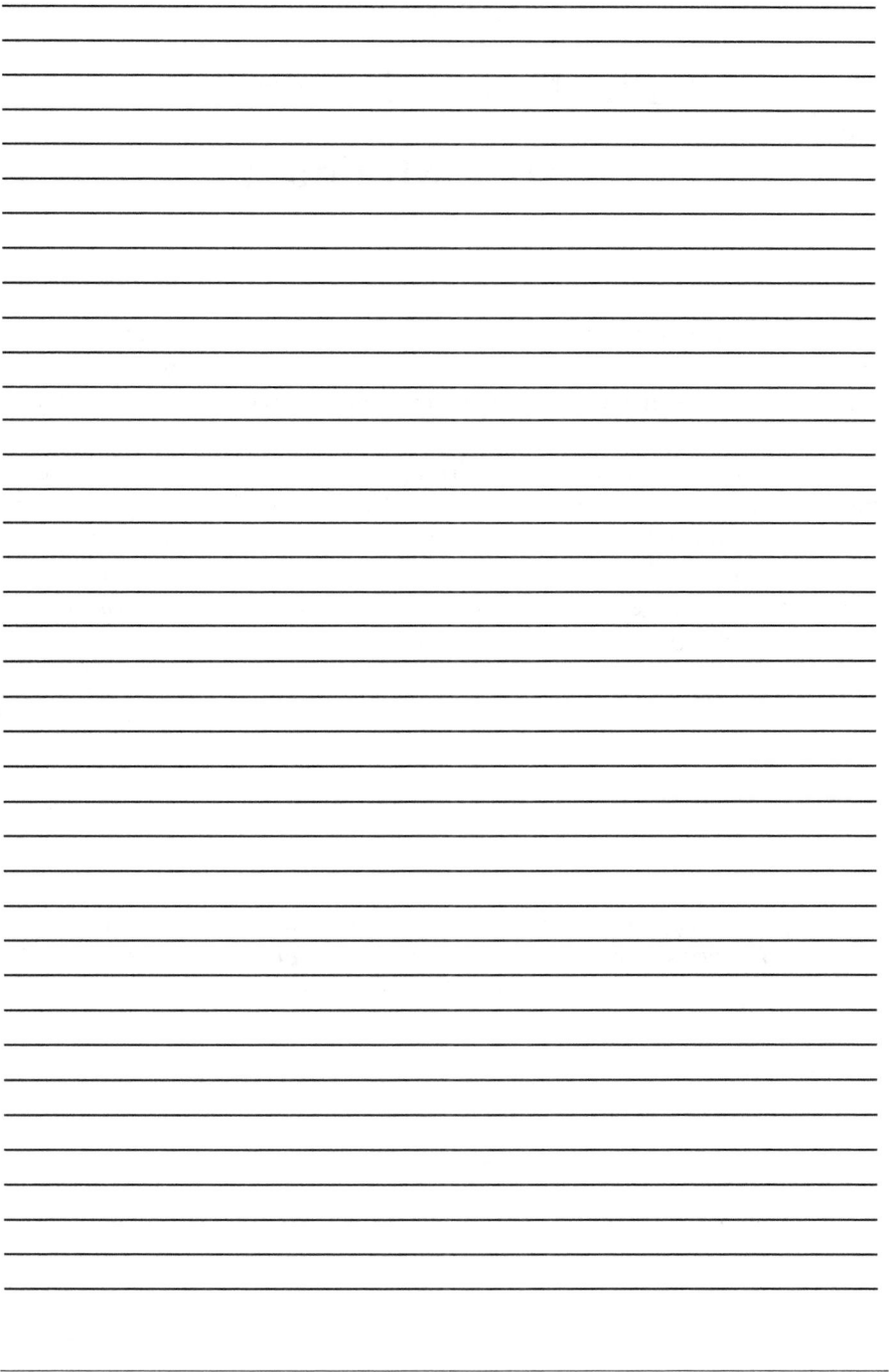

DAY 35

"The Evaluation Shift"

(Week 6 Monday)

This past weekend we had time to reflect on self and complete any tasks or challenges that were incomplete. Today evaluate where you were when you started this Refocus training and where you are today.

Take a look in depth at your progress, take inventory of the goals you have completed and executed thus far! As you do this your excitement and confidence will build and you will gain clarity as to where you stand. Then we will shift our focus to the goals that have not been completed and target them during our last week. Pat yourself on the back for all of your hard work thus far!!!

"Keep moving in the direction of your dreams. No matter how slows it may seems, stay focus, you will get to the finish line."
— Lailah Gifty Akita

Challenge # 35: Document your evaluation findings below....Make a list of the goals you have completed thus far and make a list of what has not been completed yet. Then write down why the incomplete goals haven't been completed yet and how you plan to complete them.

_____

_____

_____

_____

_____

_____

_____

_____

_____

_____

_____

_____

_____

_____

_____

_____

_____

_____

_____

_____

_____

_____

_____

_____

_____

_____

_____

_____

_____

_____

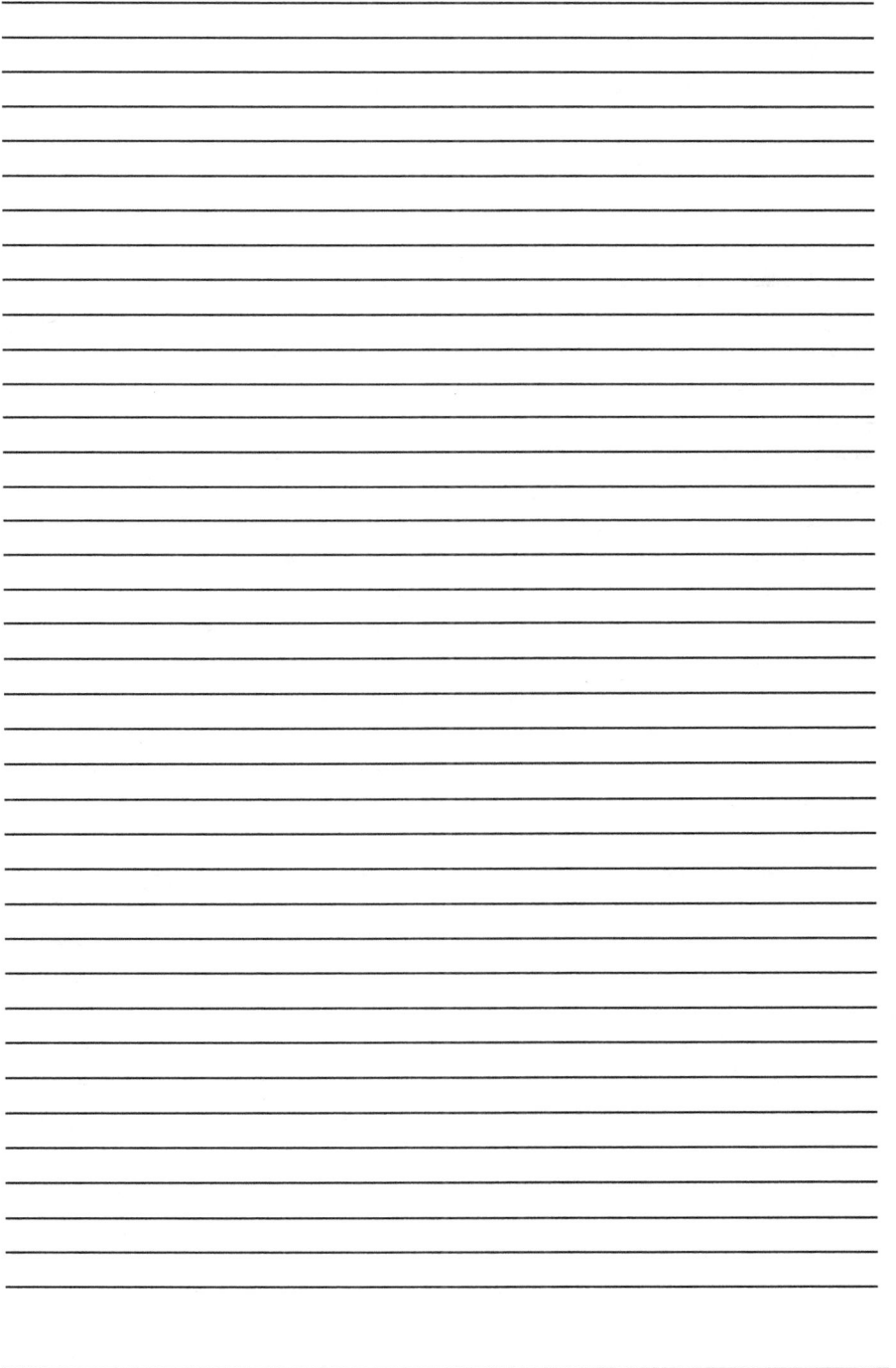

Journal

What are your thoughts?

How are you feeling?

DAY 36

"Colouring Outside the Lines"
(Week 6 Tuesday)

Don't be afraid of following your vision, executing your destiny by walking in your purpose! Be BOLD and squiggle outside the lines! Be original and authentic! Remember there is only one you! So don't be a carbon copy when you were created as the original! Everything about you is unique! You're facial features are unique, your finger prints are unique, your thoughts-they way you think is unique and your ideas are unique....Be Bold! Be Unapologetically You!!

"When I dare to be powerful, to use my strength in the service of my vision, then it becomes less and less important whether I am afraid."
— Audre Lorde

"Always be a first rate version of yourself and not a second rate version of someone else."
— Judy Garland

Challenge #36: Name 3 things that has often stopped you from following your vision or being comfortable in your skin and why? Then write an affirmation for each one listed to recite daily.

Journal

What are your thoughts?

How are you feeling?

_____
_____
_____
_____
_____
_____
_____
_____
_____
_____
_____
_____
_____
_____
_____
_____
_____
_____
_____
_____
_____
_____
_____
_____
_____
_____

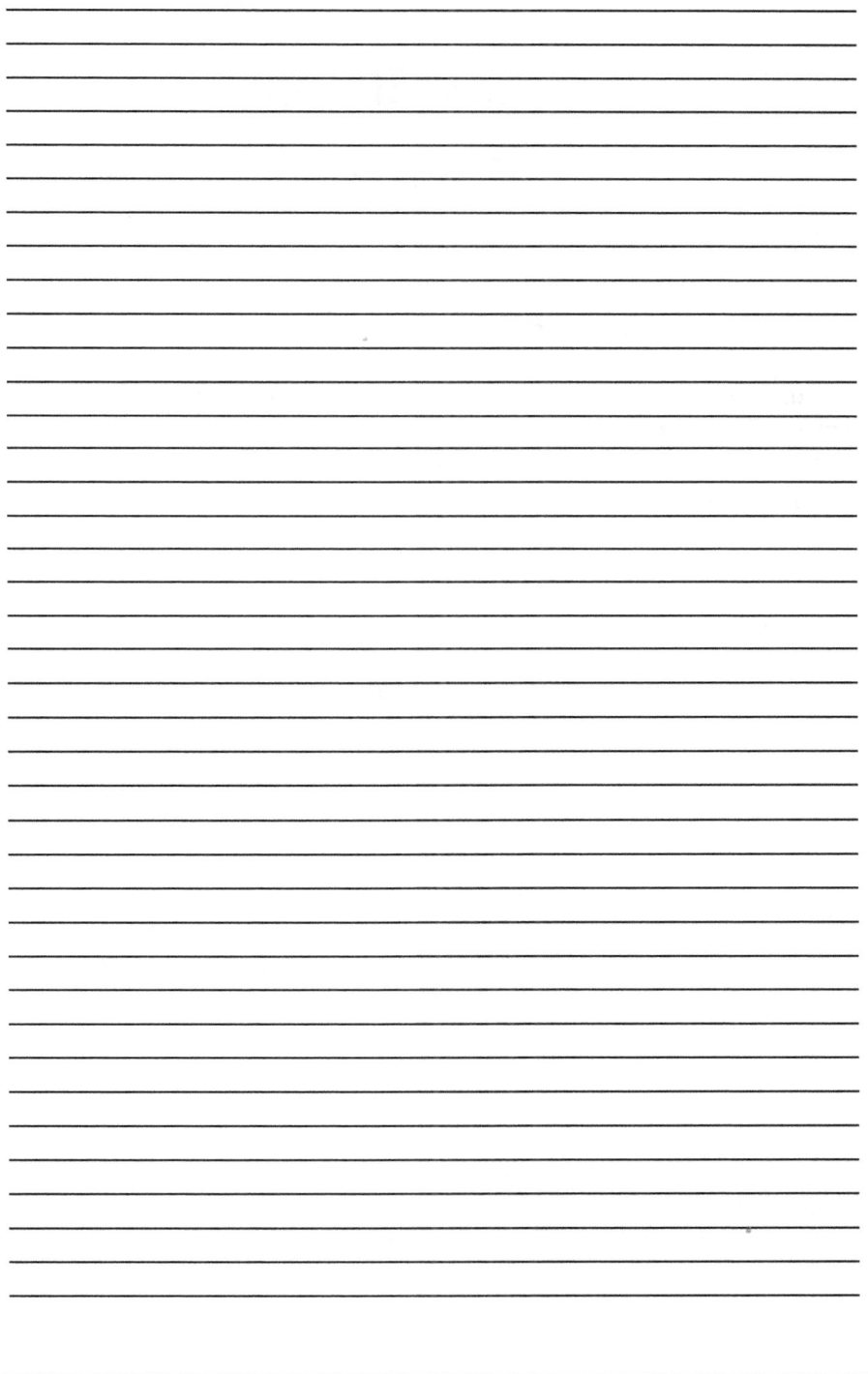

DAY 37

"Live Intentionally"
(Week 6 Wednesday)

What if I told you that most people that are successful make deliberate decisions daily geared towards their desired goals? These Decisions are not just toward business but every area of their life! Today ask yourself: Am I making choices that would catapult me in the direction that I desire to go or are my choices taking me in the opposite direction of where I desire to be?

Living intentionally also means that you don't get caught up in comparing your life business and or relationships to anybody else. Remember you were created to be an original. It is a form of distraction that if entertained will leave you feeling like you are not enough and will cause strife within self. Our competition has never been with others but with striving to be better for ourselves that we may live on purpose.

"There is nothing noble in being superior to your fellow man; true nobility is being superior to your former self."
— Ernest Hemingway

Challenge #37: Are you making choices that would catapult you in the direction that you desire to go or are your choices taking you in the opposite direction of where you desire to be?

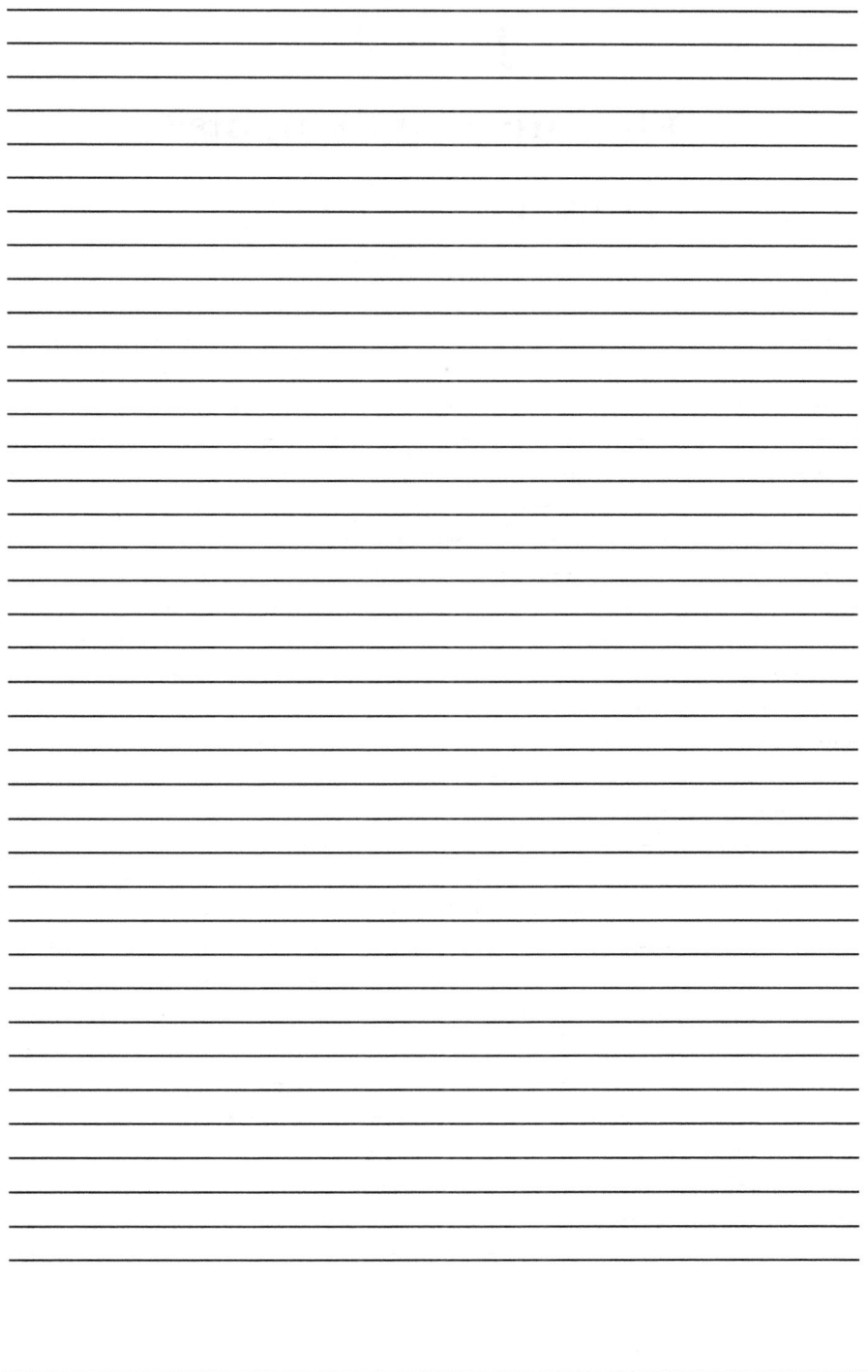

Journal

What are your thoughts?

How are you feeling?

DAY 38

"Last Moments of Clarity"
(Week 6 Thursday)

Can you see it? It's crystal clear, the new you is emerging and it looks like a new beginning for you in business, relationships, family, and spiritually! Today see you as the you, you have always desired and begin to embrace this newness! Remember that hard work does pays off and change always begins with us first!

"The beauty is that through disappointment you can gain clarity, and with clarity comes conviction and true originality."
-Conan O'Brien

Challenge #38: Write 2 things that you would like to remind the new you of in the near future in the following areas: encouragement and when under a lot of pressure. Then develop a mantra or motto that you will live by.

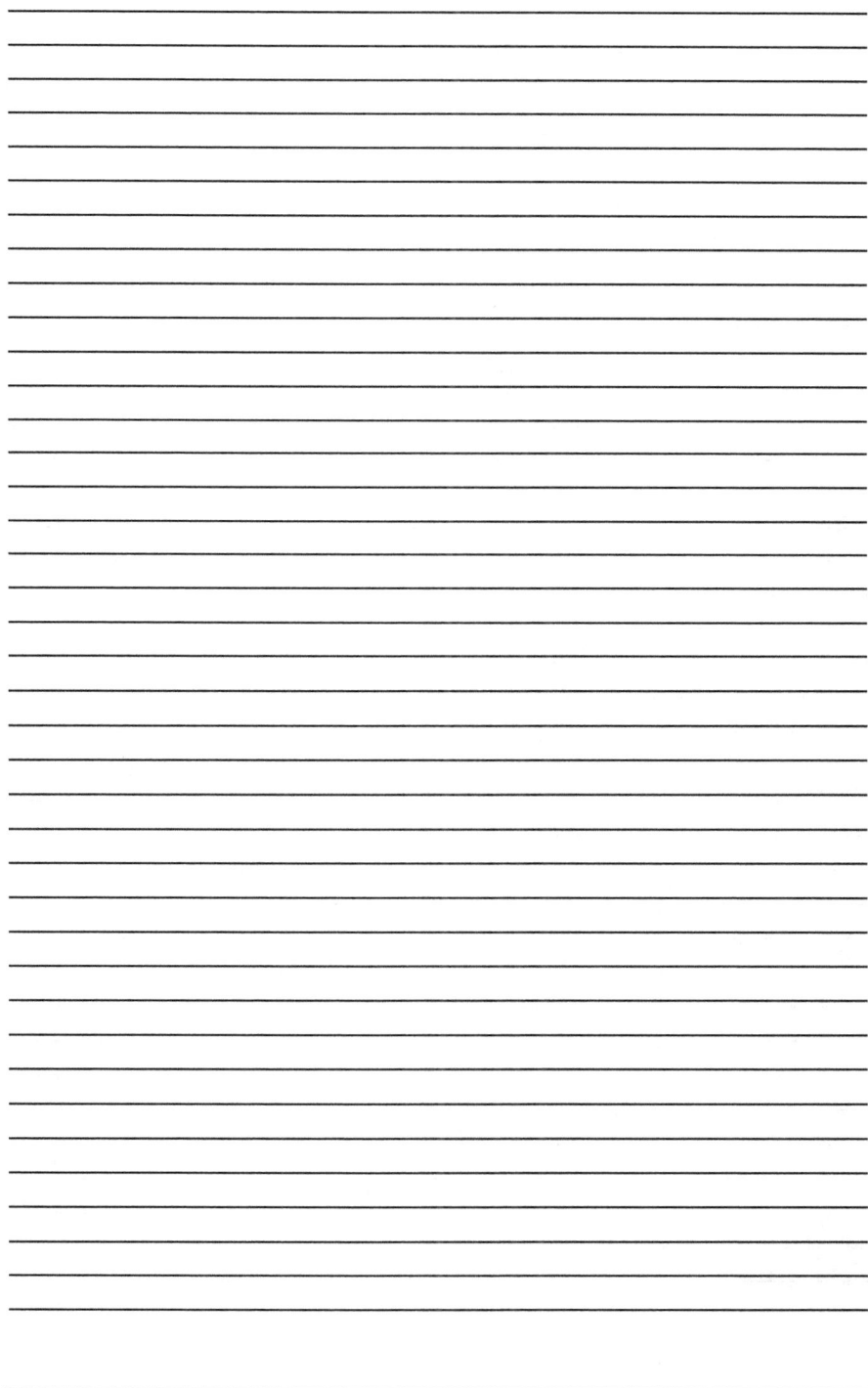

Journal

What are your thoughts?

How are you feeling?

_____
_____
_____
_____
_____
_____
_____
_____
_____
_____
_____
_____
_____
_____
_____
_____
_____
_____
_____
_____
_____
_____
_____
_____
_____
_____
_____

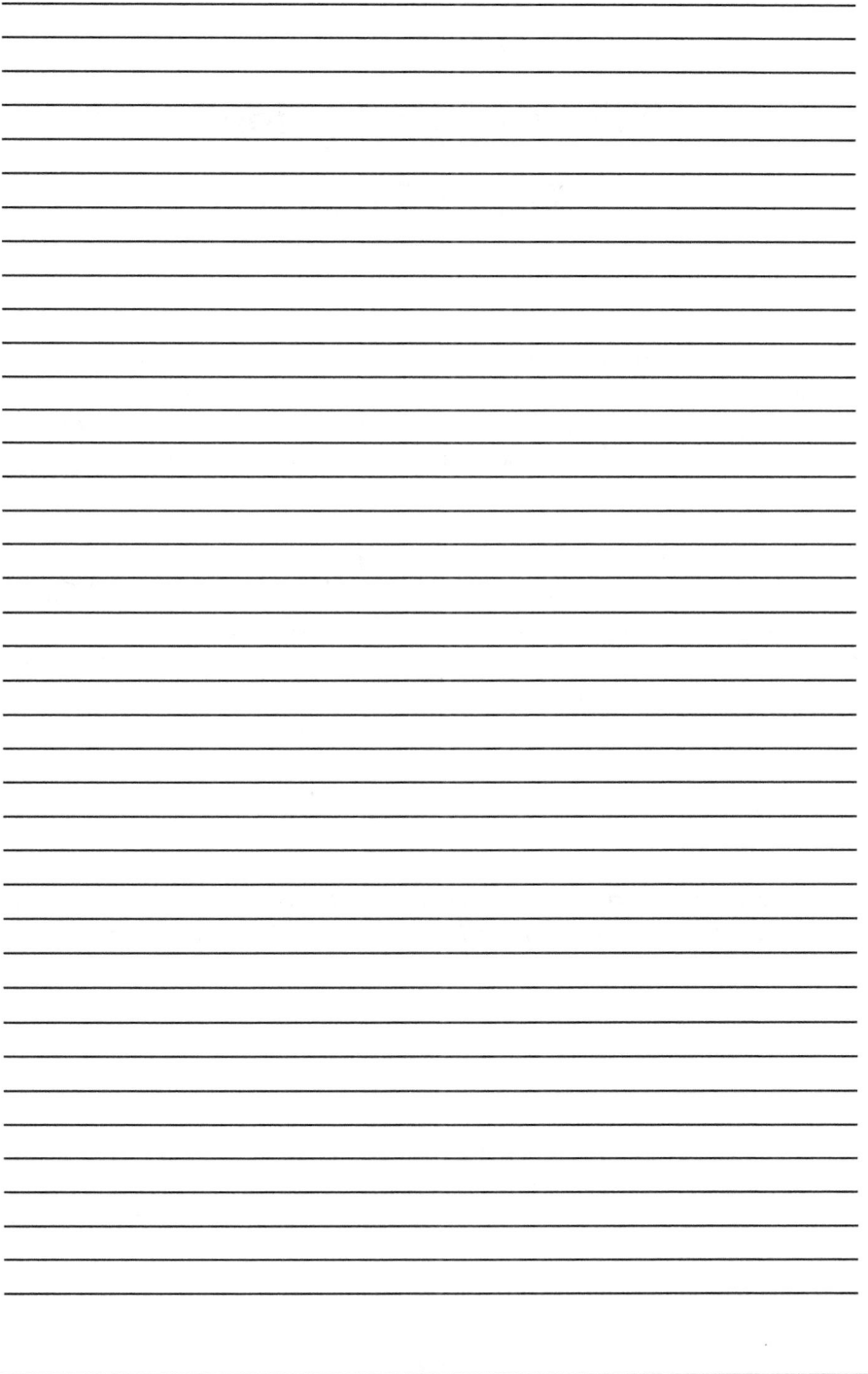

DAY 39

"Time of Reflection"
(Week 6 Friday)

For our last time of reflection we will only reflect on today Friday. Tomorrow is the last day of this personal training. Finish strong by giving all you've got! Take this time to complete any challenges you may have missed, reflect on self and or on any areas that need your attention.

Below you may journal your thoughts feelings throughout today the - this time of reflection. Just one day left! I am so happy for you! You took life by the reins, made the decision to refocus, revamp and revitalize yourself by taking action and simply doing the work. Look at all that you have accomplished!

"The real man smiles in trouble, gathers strength from distress, and grows brave by reflection." — *Thomas Paine*

Challenge #39: How does this freedom feel and in what areas of your life have you experienced freedom in? What has changed for you or in you?

_____
_____
_____
_____
_____
_____
_____
_____
_____
_____
_____
_____
_____
_____
_____
_____
_____
_____
_____
_____
_____
_____
_____
_____
_____
_____
_____
_____
_____
_____
_____
_____
_____
_____

DAY 40

"It is Finished"

(Week 6 Saturday)

I hope this 40-day personal training has helped you to refocus and reshape the areas of you that you applied it to! Look at this book as often as you need to stay accountable and continue to implement what you have learned.

You may do this training as often as you want to refocus, revamp and or revitalize yourself. With all the great work and effort that you have shown and done my friend; it is time to go back to the beginning. Yes! Answer the question below (which is remarkably similar to your first challenge) once you are done compare your answer to the first part of your answer from challenge#1 and see the difference for yourself, Outstanding right?! Growth and change are very real and tangible to those whom truly desire it!

 I would love to hear from you and how this personal training has affected your life, share your thoughts at *www.facebook.com/robyndrobbins* using the hashtag #TheRefocusChallenge

Challenge #40: Who are you today and how does this affect your day to day as well as the different areas of your life?

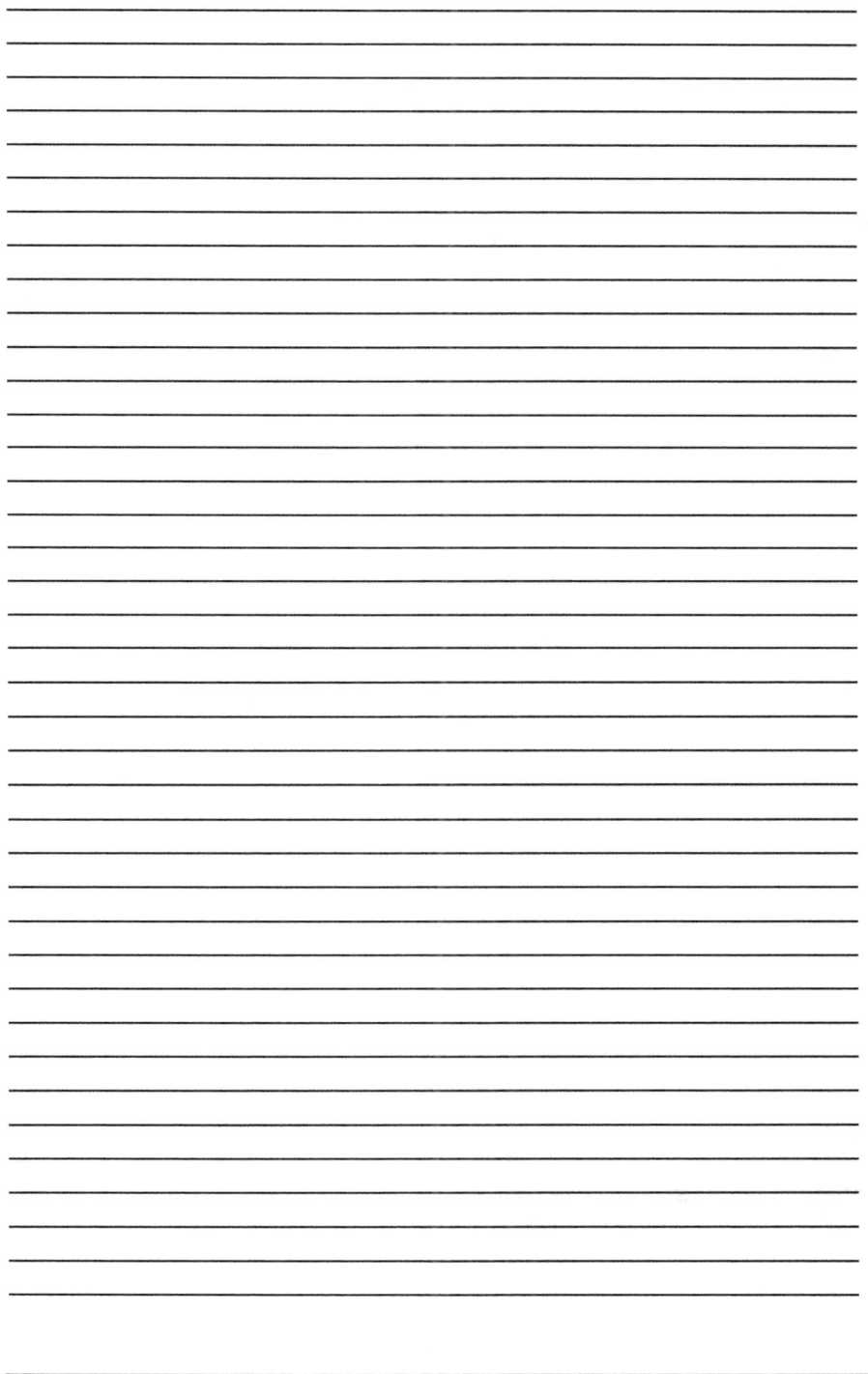

Journal

How are you feeling?

Are you confident in the work that you have done with self?

_____
_____
_____
_____
_____
_____
_____
_____
_____
_____
_____
_____
_____
_____
_____
_____
_____
_____
_____
_____
_____
_____
_____
_____
_____
_____
_____
_____

The Refocus Challenge

A 40 DAY PERSONAL TRAINING GUIDE TO

Refocus. Revamp. Revitalize

YOU

ABOUT THE AUTHOR

Robyn Robbins is a Certified Master Coach, Empowerment Teacher, thought leader and Movement Storyteller. She is the Founder & CEO of Robyn Robbins Enterprises.

Her goal is to simply add value, enrich, empower and liberate ALL that cross her path! She enjoys sharing an imparting the wisdom and knowledge she has gained through raw life experiences with others in hopes to empower them to achieve their goals and create their ideal thriving life.

In Robyn's spare time she enjoys music, the arts and the many facets of expression. She adores chic, edgy forward fashion and make-up. She loves being surrounded by family, close friends, a great meal and a good glass of red wine. Robyn loves to empower and motivate others to turn aspirations into reality, to realize and birth their dreams no matter what they have experienced in life. She calls this *Transforming Experiences.*

Learn More about Robyn Robbins Enterprises at
www.robynrobbins.com

Bulk Order Information:

Discounts are available to organizations, associations, corporations and others. Bulk orders available to U.S. trade book stores and wholesalers as well. Please contact us at the information listed below for details:

Email: info@robynrobbins.com
Office: 234-407-2477
Website: www.robynrobbins.com

Book Robyn To Speak or Coach:

Robyn has crafted powerful, eye opening and liberating talks as well as coaching curriculum that shifts the paradigm of those in attendance thus creating organic change that allows the individual to create and manifest their ideal thriving life. Some talks include but not limited to "Finding the Authentic You" and "Finding the Road to Freedom". For more on Robyn's speaking and coaching go to www.robynrobbins.com

Connect With Me Beyond the Book

I can't wait to meet you!

Facebook:
http://www.facebook.com/robyndrobbins

Instagram:
http://www.instagram.com/robyndrobbins

ClubHouse:
@RobynDRobiins

Periscope:
http://www.periscope.tv/robyndrobbins

YouTube:
www.youtube.com/channel/UCpKDYLVxjYJjdPm8cqLVlGg

One Last Thing............

If you enjoyed this book or found it useful, I'd be very grateful if you'd post a short review on Amazon. Your support really does make a difference and I read all the reviews personally so I can get your feedback and make my books even better.

If you'd like to leave a review then all you have to do is Click Here

Thank you so much in advance for your support!

Blessings & Positive Vibes,
Robyn Robbins

.

www.ingramcontent.com/pod-product-compliance
Lightning Source LLC
Chambersburg PA
CBHW070808100426
42742CB00012B/2297